BACK BENCHERS TO ACHIEVERS

DR. ARCHANA YADAV

BlueRose Publishers
New Delhi • London

First Published in December 2021

ISBN: 978-93-5472-845-7

BLUEROSE PUBLISHERS

www.bluerosepublishers.com

info@bluerosepublishers.com

+91 8882 898 898

Cover and Illustrations:

Praveen Naresh (Rahi)

Typographic Design:

Archana Yadav

Distributed by: BlueRose, Amazon, Flipkart

PREFACE

"The best brains of the nation may be found on the last benches of the classroom."

(Dr. APJ Abdul Kalam)

For the last fifteen years, I have been blessed to be around young, energetic souls full of life and dreams. I am talking about my wonderful students. I could learn to grow and become a better person on my journey with them. Some of them were already ahead in their journey of growth, some were facing a few barriers, while a few were beginning, and a few were about to begin. Those who had some obstacles to cross and needed to realize their potential, when they crossed the barriers, what a marvelous feeling it was for them, and for me to see them flourish and blossom.

Working with various institutes and students of different disciplines and levels Though there were lots of differences in different courses, different universities, student culture, and organizational culture, I found some common factors among the students who were not performing to their maximum potential. These ones were neither heroes nor very popular. They were, however, no less in potential in terms of brilliance, and intellect. What was stopping them from reaching their potential?

Mostly, the psychological barriers and preconditioning of the *mind.* They were like flower buds waiting to bloom. The only thing needed is to identify those barriers and cross them.

This is the motto and purpose of this book: to help them achieve what they want. Everyone is unique with their own package of varied preferences, intelligence, motives, drives, and ambition. Each one has his own story and is on a different journey, so it is not possible to label anyone on the basis of a few indicators. There is a lot more........... A happy, fulfilling, successful life is everyone's right. and everyone has potential. Go for it....................

Begin with me, a new journey of achievers.

....

INTRODUCTION

'Here's to the crazy ones: The misfits. The rebels. The trouble makers. The round pegs in the square holes. the ones who see things differently. They're not fond of rules. And they have no respect for the status- quo. You can quote them. disagree with them, glorify or vilify them. About the only thing you can't do is ignore them. Because they change things. They push the human race forward.
While some may see them as crazy ones, we see genius. Because the people who are crazy enough to think they can change are the ones who do" (Steve Jobs)

The term "backbencher" in this book refers to all the individuals who are not performing at the level of their best potential, just like some students who adopt behaviours of a backbencher in the classroom. To me, being a backbencher means not putting in your best effort, a half-hearted performance, an absence of enthusiasm, having a tendency to withdraw, not seeing the problem eye-to-eye, and running away from it. An attitude of "okay, fine" vs. perfection. An attitude of escapism does not yield the best results. One has to be a warrior to face the challenges, a leader who can lead his life, a captain of his own ship called life.

Even though I was not a backbencher as a student, in my own life I definitely was. After my lowest low, I decided to take charge of my own life and be my own boss. This journey was not overnight. Obviously, it took time, but it was worth it and life-changing. Today I experienced more bliss and a sense of freedom.

Free from others' destructive opinions, irrelevant judgments, being overly dependent on toxic relationships, freedom from the past, and learning the art of being in the present moment, gaining a higher level of consciousness, realizing my own strength and potential.

When my daughter was not doing academically well, I decided to work on the root cause rather than her grades. Working on her as an individual, identifying the challenges, her needs, gaps, and motivation, and filling those gaps. After a few months, results began to show, and once she was more attuned internally, happier, and higher in self-esteem, her grades automatically improved. However, my focus was on the long term and not the short term. Academic grades were short-term outcomes. In the process of building, I gave her lots of love, respect, and faith that I believed in her and assurance of unconditional support. This is a journey we are still on, getting better each day and moving towards a more fulfilling life. There is so much ahead to achieve. Once I became an achiever in my own life as a backbencher, I decided to help other people with the same.

Table of Contents

INDICATORS

Jhanvi, a nine-year-old girl in fourth grade, has been a backbencher for a few years. She consciously chooses to be the one. It is a smart choice to be a backbencher. It is a safe zone to be away from the eyes that may catch her, then embarrass her, or she may end up as a joke to others. Her classmates may laugh at her when she says something, causing anguish that suffocates her.

Being a backbencher is a relief, a saviour from pain, and a day is saved from being ruined because of that experience of humiliation, being inferior, unworthy, an idiot, or a joke. "What a relief!" The teacher did not notice me, and took a sigh of relief, whispering to Gauri, who sat next to her, that being in the company of not-so-smart kids like her made her feel safe and unthreatened.

Reshu, a second-year undergraduate student, occupied one of the last benches as usual. Due to his inability to speak fluently, he avoided his turn to speak in front of the class, so that it saved him from being ridiculed.

Anjana, a fifth-grader, did not do her homework. Out of fear of getting scolded and to save herself from embarrassment in front of her peers, she chose to occupy the last row. It became a habit. The "free-zone" at the backbenches is enjoyed, celebrated, and lived. it is also accompanied by a fear of being caught, a feeling of guilt about being a thief also exists. Fear is the dominant factor among the backbenchers; *fear of rejection, shame, humiliation, and pain failing.*

> **Fear of rejection, shame, humiliation the agony of failure are the dominant factors among backbenchers.**

Due to fear of failing, we miss a lot in life. It applies even more to kids who are sensitive, who perceive themselves as less than others, and who think their chances of success are weak They know they have often failed expectations of people around them, such as parents, teachers, siblings, peers, etc., and don't want to repeat that experience. It brings guilt. It brings pain. Even though they want to shine like stars like their siblings, classmates, or friends, the pain of not being one of them is less than the pain of failing their people over and over. How easy is that calculation?

"A person who never made a mistake never tried anything new" (Albert Einstein)

WITHDRAWAL

An attitude of withdrawal is often found among such students. Eventually, the same attitude affects them in other domains of life also. They grow up to be adults who make half-hearted efforts and do not strive to achieve their full potential. Students often display withdrawal behaviors in the class, avoiding participation in in-class activities, taking initiative, or doing things for the heck of it, which eventually leads to taking shortcuts in attaining goals.

> **There are no shortcuts to a happy, blissful, and successful life.**

"You are braver than you believe. You are stronger than you feel and smarter than you think." (Christopher Robin)

Students who do not take enough interest in class are also found to be veteran procrastinators. Not doing the homework, not preparing well in advance for an exam or test. When you're late for the school bus, the goal is to put it off as long as possible. Procrastination is a habit, an attitude, or behavior that costs one dearly all their life, in all domains of life.

The root cause associated with it is later explained in the section of causes. When we postpone things for the future that should be done now, we cut down on the most important resource: time. We do not meet our deadlines. Even if we do, it is not with perfection or done with our best effort.

People stop relying on or investing in relationships with such people. One of the groups of students in my class regularly misses the deadline for submitting the assignment. Same group, same people. They want to keep pushing as long as possible. The same kids who have grown up to be adults are still procrastinators.

A Case of a financial analyst

A financial analyst who was very competent and intelligent but was having problems at work because of her procrastination habits. It affects the quality of life of an individual, his relationships, and his work. After many sessions, she eventually learned to cope with it.

The underlying cause was the fact that she did not value her time and the things associated with her. The deeper cause was that she did not value herself enough, having lower self-worth. Procrastination is not just an attitude, habit, or behavior; it reflects deeper issues that need to be tackled to fix life.

> *"Procrastination is one of the most common and deadliest diseases. Its toll on success and happiness is heavy."*
>
> Wayne Gretzky

FINDING SHORTCUTS IS A SIMPLER METHOD

Choices made to choose an easier way out, avoiding the pain of learning, are shortcuts, not a legitimate way to fix a problem. A person who takes the pain to come out of their comfort zone, adapt, and update the map will grow. Success and a life of prosperity are not possible with the easier shortcuts in life.

They may be temporary solutions or temporary illusions of solutions, but they are not a road that leads to success. If you know a strong personality or a successful person, there is a story about their endless efforts, the pain they have endured, the sacrifices they have made, and the learning from many failed attempts before arriving where they are now from where they were. ....

Move out of your

comfort zone,

ABSENTEEISM

Absenteeism is an indicator of the behavior of something we are not motivated by, not fond of, something we want to avoid but have to do out of compulsion or when there is no other way out. We, adults, make excuses to attend an event organized by people we are really comfortable with.

We make excuses for our absence, or even if we go, it has to be as quick as possible. The same goes for students who are not motivated enough to go to a school or classroom. If a class is online and network issues are a permanent problem, their instruments, such as laptops, tabs, and mobile phones, break more frequently, especially on the day of a test, exam, or assignment.

When they finally make it, their presence is only physical, not mental, as their minds are wandering to where something of their interest lies. It has become easier with online classes; just join the class, turn off your camera, play games on your phone, chat on WhatsApp, and when your name is called, abruptly leave the class, claiming a network problem. Join back when it is safe again, either today or tomorrow.

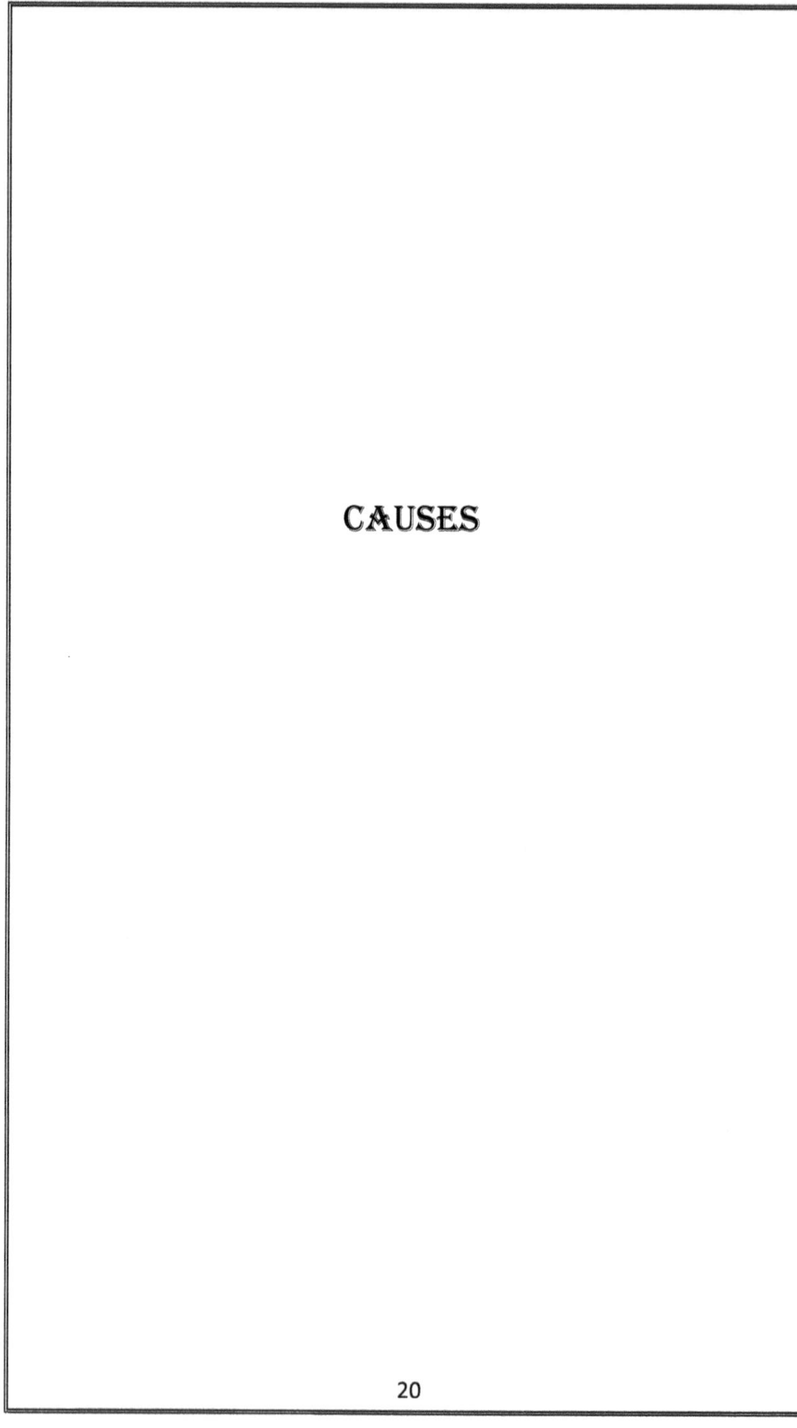

CAUSES

LOW SELF-ESTEEM

My daughter, when she was in first grade, had a new admission, on the first day of school she was very excited about her new school, expecting to have new friends and have a lot of fun. She was an extrovert and loved making friends. When she asked her teacher for permission to go to the washroom to pee more than once, her teacher scolded her very badly.

She was terrified of her angry gestures and rough tone. From that, she started holding it in fear that the teacher might scold her. One day, she could not hold it and peed in her pants. Her peers teased her. From that day, she avoided interaction with peers. After being scolded for every trivial thing, she decided to keep mum. Later, it became her habit and her behavior in the classroom. One day, she was terrified because the teacher had told students in the class that she would cut their fingers if they did not write well. She believed in it. As a result, she developed a negative attitude toward her school and class, as well as low self-esteem and self-confidence in herself.

It was an international school of good repute, despite my making numerous attempts to get in touch with the teacher and principal in vain. Finally, I changed schools. This time I took a lot of time to decide on it and did a lot of research. It has been two years since then, and though there are improvements, I am still working.

I noticed similar issues at playschool, particularly among the female caretakers who take kids to the washroom and help them on the school bus. If their behavior is harsh, especially sensitive children, are negatively impacted. It may not be noticed immediately, but it will reflect on the personality in the long term for sure.

My friend has two daughters; one is fair and the other one is dark-skinned. The one with fair skin is an extrovert, while the one with dark skin is an introvert. Both are very talented. But the one who is fair-skinned gets a lot of attention while the other one is ignored. Sometimes, she feels even her parents, relatives, and cousins behave with the same bias. She is too young to evaluate her own worth at this age; all she knows is that She is not important to others, which she contemplates as she is not important enough. She has become a procrastinator and attempts things half-heartedly.

She would join a hobby course, leave it half done, and move to another, not giving her best. M. Scott Peck mentions one of the cases of his patients, a financial analyst. Despite being efficient and competent, she had a habit of procrastination. Due to feeling unimportant.

> Low self-esteem is like driving a car with the hand brake on.
>
> Maxwel Mlatz.

SELF-CONCEPT

How do we perceive ourselves? What we think about ourselves is the most important thing. We can pretend or lie to others, but we can't lie to ourselves.

The self-concept of a person is very crucial to a happy, successful, fulfilling life. A person with a poor self-concept does not associate himself with pride. He feels he is not good enough, which determines his self-esteem, which impacts self-efficacy, and eventually his achievements and goals in life.

Sanjana had a string of failed relationships in which she would put herself in the backseat and play the nurturing and self-sacrifice roles, justifying why she was not receiving the same in return. Despite leaving no stone unturned to make the relationship work, when she was dumped, she would try to figure out what mistake she made. She would hold him responsible for every such event. She would evaluate it as her failure.

In order to retain a relationship, she would be under constant pressure to please the other person. Approval from others became very significant to her. She would accept this failure as "she did not deserve him" or "I'm not good enough," or "I'm not that bright, happening, beautiful, cool, interesting. "Self-concept leaves imprints in all domains of life, not just academics. What view one has about himself is crucial because it is deeply rooted in the subconscious mind and needs reprogramming, new conditioning of the mind with a new message. How to go about those techniques is mentioned in the Remedies section.

> **Self-concept leaves imprints in all domains of life not just in academics**

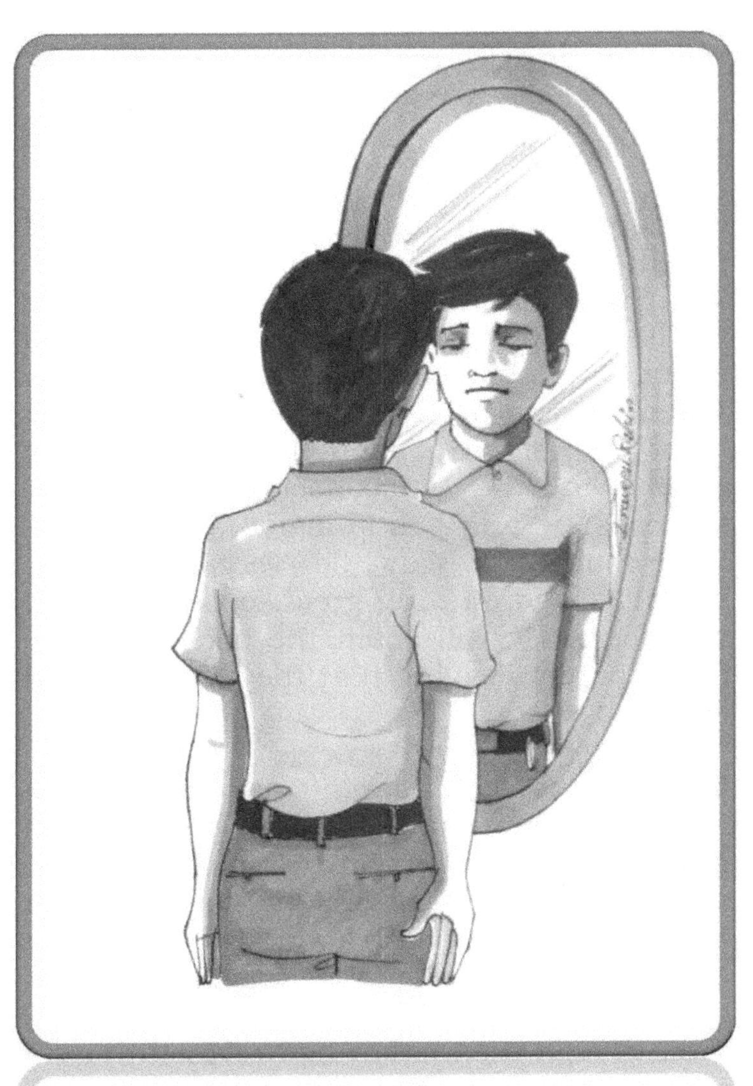

Build a Positive self-image

PERSONALITY DEVELOPMENT

***Parents* or caregivers** in a child's childhood have a huge role in the personality development of a child. A child looks at his parents like God. His family is his world. What comes from his parents is his ultimate truth? At a very young age, he is not rational enough to question, analyze, or evaluate. When he gets a message from his parents, "you are not good enough." It settles very deeply in the subconscious and later becomes an automated behavior. Communication may be verbal or non-verbal. Children are great observers and absorbers. He will catch the body language of his parents saying that they are ashamed of him.

Middle-class Indian parents assume scolding and beatings are normal; it makes the child disciplined, an illusion which is due to unawareness. I was in the local market when I noticed a girl about five years old crying bitterly. Her mother was slapping her over and over. She had asked for a toy again, even though the mother had refused. It gave the mother the right to beat her in the market, and everyone around me took it very normally. It is okay if a mother can beat her daughter in public and a husband can beat his wife secretly at home. How very acceptable; what is wrong with that? Really? this is an accepted, unsaid notion that needs rectification if the mental health of the next generation is to be wished for. I could not bear the sight anymore and decided to go to her and intervene. Even though she stopped beating her there, I am sure her behaviour would be repeated later. Imagine the psychological damage of such kids who receive no respect from parents; for many parents, the concept of respecting a child seems very alien.

Once, when I went for a walk outside my apartment society, I noticed that there was a small market nearby where a semi-rural crowd often came to shop. While going back, I heard a woman shouting at a child, "laughing, I will kick you." I turned to see them and noticed a girl of about six years old, smitten in fear, turning her head low. The smile had vanished. As if she had committed a crime by laughing at her mother. I asked the mother, "whose child is this? She answered, "mine only" in a tone as if it were so unfortunate. I said, "Is this the way you speak to your child?" She ignored me and pretended to behave as if I was invisible. What kind of personality and self-concept can be expected from the girl when she grows up? When her own mother shows no respect to her, how in the world is she going to respect herself and develop high self-esteem and a healthy personality?

The case might be a little different than the so-called more educated ones, a little more affluent in english, wearing branded clothes and maintaining sophisticated manners. They are so busy in children's competitions as if they are going to fail. They want to keep their heads high in the race for supremacy by putting too much pressure on children, even though they are incapable of withstanding it. A colleague of mine, who is rich and comes from an educated family, is often seen in anxiety if his child scores even a few marks lower than his peers or does not secure the first position in any activity, competition, or participation.

He brags proudly about it. He also complains that my child is getting timid and shrinking in his cell, but his highly ambitious and competitive mind is focused on winning, not on the child's emotional health.

According to him, if his child secures second rank in the class, it means he is second, or if the child fails, it means he has failed. In order to keep your head high in your circle, your child has to be number one, because then you are number one. How could a mature parent's ego depend on the performance of the child?

Dr. M. Scott Peck, In his best-selling book, *"The Road Less Travelled,"* psychiatrist discusses how complexes are formed due to flawed parenting. He mentions the two most common complexes as "character disorder" and "neuroses." Character disordered people are those who do not assume any responsibility for their actions, while neurotic people assume too much responsibility. Children of character disorder parents often have neuroses.

> *The two most common complexes as "Character Disorder" and "Neuroses. Character Disordered people are those who do not assume any responsibility for their actions ,while neurotic people assume too much responsibility.*

The Case of an individual who had an Inability to Trust

There is an interesting case about a man who developed an inability to trust; he could not stick to a job for more than six months, damning his boss and the people around him. He had great difficulty in maintaining relationships, especially through trust issues. On deeper probation, it was revealed that in his childhood, his parents would forget to keep their promises; they sometimes even forgot to pick him up from school; they promised a bike on his birthday but forgot about it.

Such parental behaviors caused hurt and pain to the child. In order to save himself from pain, he learned a method to not trust his parents. No trust, no pain. It was his conditioning at a deeper level. As an adult, he did not trust people around him. For a child, his parents are his world. What they do is how things are done. Such complexes are reflected in the behaviors of children and adults.

Daniel Goleman, in his book Emotional Intelligence, explains that the Amygdala (responsible for emotional memory) is fully developed at the birth of the child, while the Neocortex (part of the human brain's Cerebral Cortex responsible for cognitive functioning) develops much later. That is why emotional experiences of childhood are deeply settled subconsciously and contribute to many perceptions, beliefs, attitudes, and behaviours later on.

Then comes the rare breed of wise ones who understand the child, accept him, support him unconditionally, and assure him we are around irrespective of anything. You do your best, we will do ours. We will not be ashamed of you if you cannot score more marks than your friend or my colleague's neighbour's child. We would go as per our strength and speed.

They try to find the cause if a child is not performing academically or adopting a withdrawal attitude. If he is bullied, or whatever the cause is, with patience, give him time to work by himself. who understands that a child was not born overnight, so no change is possible overnight. Things take time. Strong parenting, which helps the child to accept and respect himself, Parents who help a child develop a rational mind that does not take garbage randomly thrown in the form of opinions, judgments, and comments that is not constructive.

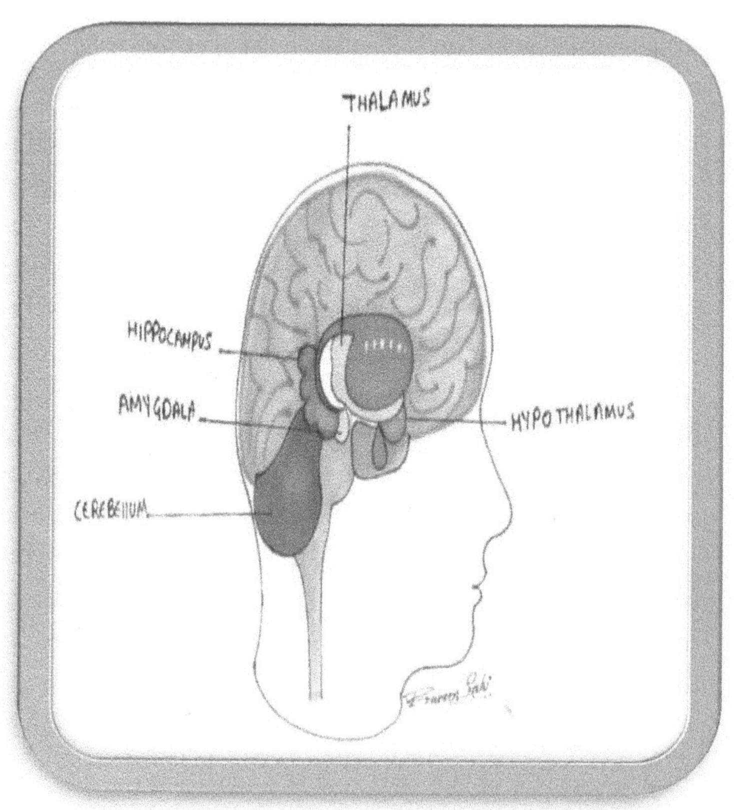

- Hippocampus: Responsible for storing dry facts, Information in the brain

- Amygdala: A limbic system structure in the brain responsible for emotional memories

- Thalamus: A structure within the brain, like traffic police, also called a relay station

- Sensory receptors send information to Thalamus and Thalamus transmits information to Cerebellum.

In infants, the Amygdala is almost fully developed at birth. While the Hippocampus (crucial for narrative memory information) and Neocortex (seat of rational thought) are not fully formed, early life experiences and emotional experiences based on contact between infants and caregivers are so powerful and yet so difficult to interpret from an adult's point of view because they are stored in the Amygdala as rough, wordless blueprints for emotional life. These memories from the earliest childhood are created at a time before infants have words for their experience.

Amygdala (Emotional Memory) –matures very early.In infants, the Amygdala is almost fully developed at birth. While the Hippocampus (crucial for narrative memory information) and Neocortex (seat of rational thought) are not fully formed, early life experiences and emotional experiences based on contact between infants and caregivers are so powerful and yet so difficult to interpret from an adult's point of view because they are stored in the Amygdala as rough, wordless blueprints for emotional life. These memories from the earliest childhood are created at a time before infants have words for their experience. Later in life, these emotional memories are triggered when we are confused or surprised by our emotional outbursts.

TEACHERS

https://fb.watch/9jglDQFf74/

Teachers play a role in self-concept, especially in early school. Often, they do not realize the influence they have on their students. A student who is embarrassed in front of his peers and believes he is not good enough will never be good enough; it is not his belief that empowers the mind and becomes the teacher's self-fulfilling prophecy. I remember a group of three girls in my class who failed every year. Most of the teachers treated them with disgust, looking them down. One of them even claimed that he could guarantee that they would fail this year too, and it came true. Out of empathy, I decided to interact with them, get friendly with them, and help them. After interacting with them, I found nothing wrong with their intellect. The biggest hurdle was their own belief now, which was earlier others' belief. Now two strong belief systems of others and one of their own are working in the same direction with greater force and results ought to come in the direction they were made.

My daughter, who was very confident and social, suddenly turned very fearful and She disliked her school. On grilling, I found out it was her teacher's behaviour that had created a hostile classroom climate and that she would often scold harshly. So much so, she was not allowed to go pee, often being turned down and scolded. As a result, she started holding back in fear. Her confidence was dipping gradually. She was not doing academically well, and some teachers make it very difficult for children who need a hand to climb up; they would rather push them further down. I changed her school and took the appropriate measures. Things got better over time.

I had great teachers, which played a significant role in my personality developing into a confident one. In my recent research on undergraduate students, it was revealed that the teacher's behaviour and classroom climate affect the self-esteem of students and eventually impact their academic performance, as well as other domains of life and eventual achievements in life. It was found that for students' free communication, where they can express their views without fear or shame, the teacher's demonstration of unbiased behaviour, the teacher's attitude towards students, motivation, and acceptance of the student mattered a great deal to students in relation to their self-esteem.

<u>https://fb.watch/9jglDQFf74/</u>

The given link is a video of a child psychologist who went through emotional trauma and a nervous breakdown due to the behaviours of her teachers and who later chose to become a child therapist, helping children to cope and also creating awareness about how teachers can play a crucial role in the personality development of the child. Do watch it.

The opinions of one's peers are extremely important. When it affects adults so much, how much more would it affect children who are far more sensitive? When a child is not accepted well in his peer group, they gradually adopt a docile role.

In adolescents, acceptance from the opposite gender plays a significant role. As a result, they try too hard to please the group leader or other group members in order to become part of the group, or they start avoiding them altogether and become loners.

A Panchtantra story about four Friends.

Four friends decide to go to the city for a better life. One of them had gone to the city and was very well educated. The other two also had some skills, but one of them, according to the group, was not as skilled as the other three. In the night, while on the journey, passing through the forest, they decided to rest in the forest under a tree and resume the journey in the morning. One of them was very learned and knew spells, and claimed that by casting a spell of knowledge, he could bring the lion back to life; the other two agreed; and the fourth, while not as learned, asked his friends not to do so, fearing that the lion, once resurrected, would devour them. Those who were enthusiastic, on the other hand, did not stop. The one who knew how to cast spells used his spell, and the others followed suit. The fourth one participated actively, while the fourth one did not join them but rather climbed the tree. Once the spell was over, the lion came back to life and devoured all of them. Only the so-called idiot saved his life. because life demonstrated who was an idiot. was assertive in his own way. Though he was alone, he followed his instinct and saved his life.

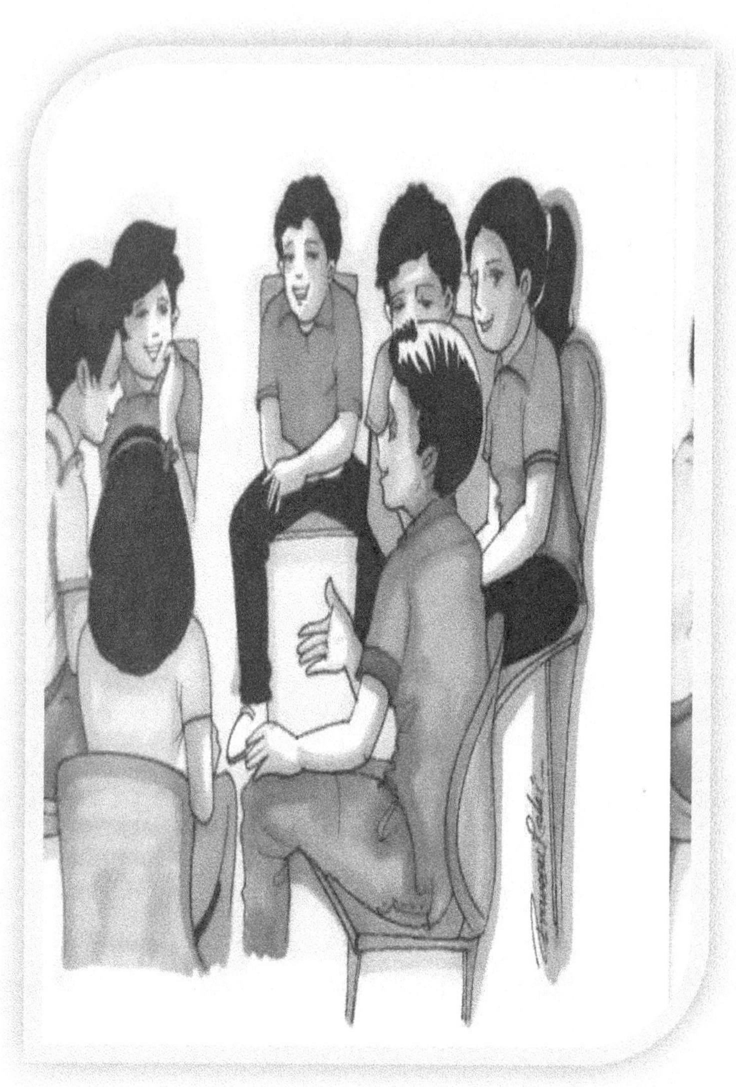

"*The higher you rise above your fears the higher you will rise above your peers.*"(Matshona Dhliwayo)

III. REMEDIES

BEGIN your journey Today, now

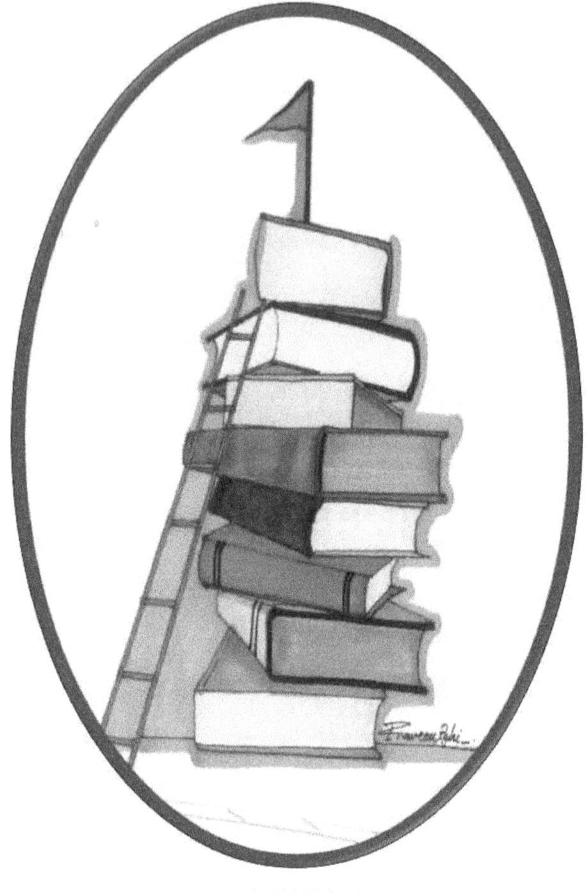

Self-acceptance is the foundation of a healthy personality. One who is unable to accept himself is unable to accept others. Self-acceptance is regarded as the first component of emotional intelligence. Accepting and Respecting Your Body Whether you are fair or dark, tall or short, fat or thin.

The very first thing closest to us, our first identity, is our body. Who decides the norms? Some beauty contests are commercial companies whose sheer motive is to earn a profit, even at the cost of one's self-worth. So one's weaknesses would be exploited to the maximum till the weakness is transformed into strength.

In particular, girls grow up with the belief system that they have no choice but to look a certain way, as defined by some. Through fairy tales, it is in their subconscious that one day a prince will come to rescue them. They will get a good match if they look within the defined criteria, so even a very bright girl may develop a complex if she is not fair or thin. Instead of being proud and focusing on her talents, her focus shifts to fit in with the illusion image.

You are you. Accept and respect your uniqueness. There is no need to be or not be like anyone else. Even the drives and motivations of identical twins may be different. Accept your limitations and respect them. Dr. Abdul Kalam is known for his brilliance, not for his hairstyle or looks. What if he was judged on illusion beauty parameters? Steve Jobs is known for his out-of-the-box thinking, not for his interpersonal relationships. Everyone has their own limitations and blessings. We lose sight of our blessings and begin judging ourselves in the same way that others do. Stop judging yourself in the same way that others do

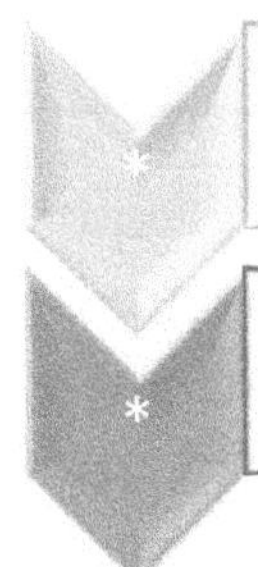

- You are your own master.

- Your life's designer and architech.

Either you are you, or you are nothing. Everyone wants the original; nobody wants a fake or lookalike. You cannot enjoy being anyone's shadow; you can never reach your own full potential unless you are yourself. Be comfortable in your own skin, respect your individuality, and Be the best version of yourself.

BE KIND TO YOURSELF.

Be true to yourself the way you expect your best relationship or that person to be. When you value someone, you want to get to know the person, respect him, spend time with him, and forgive him. You do not make him feel petty for his mistakes; rather, you provide support when he falls, encouragement when needed, and most importantly, you don't see him with other people's lenses but with your own. You pamper the person with valuable gifts. We cannot blame others for being unkind to us if we ourselves don't bother to look after ourselves.

When was the last time you pampered yourself? How long do you punish yourself with low opinion and guilt for a mistake, big or small, made?

Do not be a dust bin to others.

Do not keep others' garbage (judgments, opinions, comments, etc.). How conveniently do we accept others' opinions without checking the facts about us? Are you a dustbin? Or a human being?

Garbage is meant to be thrown in the dustbin, not treasured in the locker forever. Others' judgments, misconceptions, low opinions, are garbage. They threw it at you. Dust it off and move on, or wash your clothes (soul) and keep moving. We have a choice, but how long will it take? and how do we decide to treasure the garbage? It may be with a purpose to tear you down, hiding your own fears, or maybe unintentional due to carelessness or lack of knowing all the facts. How much time does it take to pass judgment on somebody? It is effortless. It takes a lot of effort to get to know somebody, to be in their shoes. How many do that? The reason could be anything, but not worth enough to waste our precious resources like time, energy, and thought on it.

MANAGE EFFECTIVELY POWERS OF SUBCONSCIOUS MIND

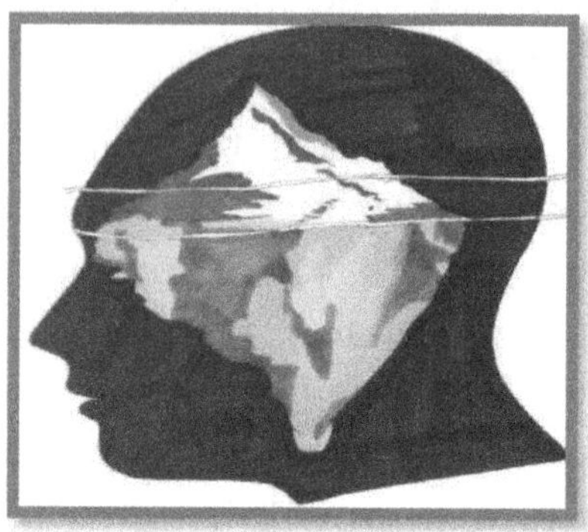

The conscious mind is concerned with current awareness and working memory, which includes short-term memory, awareness of the world around us, and awareness of ourselves. Making judgments, thinking, rationalizing. We are aware of how to behave in the classroom and during conversations. It is active as long as we are awake.

Even though there is no geographical division, it is still that part of the brain that is active all the time and never sleeps. It is on duty 24*7. It keeps working without a break, like breathing. Whatever information is received by the subconscious, it absorbs it as it is and executes it with all its power, aligning with the powers of the universe and nature. It is many times more powerful than the conscious brain. It has no moral compass, no judgment. It has unlimited storage for information. As a result, depending on how we use it, execution may be in our best or worst interests.

Sometimes people feel frustrated that they are not able to give up an addiction, despite trying their best to give up anger, reactions, unfavourable behaviors, or are unable to form habits that they want. It's not that they don't want it consciously; they wish and want to be able to do so due to subconscious conditioning.

We all have our own reactive triggers in certain situations. We are unaware of why we end up with those reactions that we don't want to have. People have changed their lives for the better from the bad, made dreams come true, vanished their life's problems, and switched to a happy, fulfilling, successful life by effectively using techniques of the subconscious mind.

Let's learn how to tap its powers in our best interest and transform our lives from where we are to where we want to be.

Whatever you want to have or achieve, say it to yourself as many times as possible.

Remember to say the opposite of what you are not currently doing but want to be. I want to be a topper in your class/boards. Say I am the topper of my class/board. Or if you want to be successful, say, "I am successful, or I am rich, or powerful. Remember to recite it in the present tense. Say that with conviction. These recitations will be taken by the subconscious mind. The brain does not distinguish between wish and reality, truth and lie; it simply accepts and executes the instructions as they are.

> **The brain dose not distinguish between wish and reality ,truth and lie; it simple accepts the instruction/inform action and executes it as is.**

"The Power of Your Subconscious Mind," Dr. Joseph Murphy narrates a case of a woman who started reciting in reverse, "My memory from today is improving." By three weeks, her memory had come back to normal. And in numerous cases where he worked, marvelous results occurred in healing and fulfilling life, from poor to rich. Similarly, Vex King, in his book, supports the techniques and power of the subconscious mind.

> Before going to bed and after waking up, when the mind is at its most powerful and clean as a slate, feed your message without fail. In fact, prayer is a technique for the subconscious mind.

Before going to bed and after waking up, when the mind is at its most powerful and clean as a slate, feed your message without fail. In fact, prayer is a technique for the subconscious mind.

When my daughter was facing low self-esteem issues, I decided to use the affirmation technique. She was very fearful and related herself to negative labels. So much so that she would frequently make negative statements about herself, and when complimented, she would argue that it was not appropriate in her case. In order to fix this, I began using words for her that were the opposite of what she was currently saying but would like to be. In the beginning, when I would tell her, "you are so beautiful and smart," she would argue

arguing. Then I gave her a week's worth of chocolate if she didn't say anything negative about herself. She met her goal and received a reward, and I continued it for a month.

She stopped empowering her mind with low-quality information about herself. It was our first step to triumph. In the next step, I gave her the target to repeat affirmations after waking up, before going to sleep, and during the daytime whenever possible, statements like "I am powerful, beautiful, smart." When we began, she was doing very poorly in academics and had developed a withdrawal behaviour that was very inactive, sometimes even aggressive. Today, she is doing very well in all domains, not just academics.

DON'Ts

- Stop saying negative words to you immediately, such as
- I am unable to do it.
- I FEAR
- I am not good enough.
    - I am not intelligent.

Even in a joke, the subconscious mind does not know the difference. It will take the information as it is and execute it. Quit using negative vocabulary. Don't repeat such negative vocabulary, even in your thoughts. Thoughts are powerful.

Quit using negative vocabulary

A picture is worth a thousand words.

The mind understands this principle very well and responds to it in a miraculous way. Visualization is yet another powerful subconscious mind technique. See yourself in the scene in detail, as if you are living it. The mind believes in it and executes it. If you want to be the topper of the class, imagine who you are. Imagine all the scenes that will come to pass. Live the moment in your brain now. If you want to be successful, visualize yourself as you are. You can even place the related pictures in front of you to help you visualize. In his book, "The Power of the Sub-Conscious Mind," Joseph Murphy reveals in numerous cases how it has helped.

When I was struggling with my life, with few resources and no means to continue my studies, but I had a dream to have the life that I deserved, to have a career, to be an independent woman, and to live a life of respect, I knew in my mind that my current life was not my destiny; I didn't know how, but I knew my life was not this. But I used to picture in my mind what I wanted without even knowing that I was practicing a technique of the sub-conscious mind.

It works irrespective of good or bad, knowing or not knowing. The subconscious mind cannot rationalize; it executes what is being fed to it. My life completely changed by taking a small step slowly and gradually. I had no idea about the sub-conscious mind's abilities at the time. People judged me, criticized me. It was very difficult. I grew up in a middle-class orthodox family of five children, did not attend a reputable college, and did not have any proper qualifications, but things changed miraculously. At times, I felt some divine power was assisting me, setting my path with perfection. Now that I am aware of how to use the powers within, I also know what not to do. Because I didn't know how to use my mental powers, I received both the best and worst gifts in life.

☆ ☆ Wake up early ☆ ☆

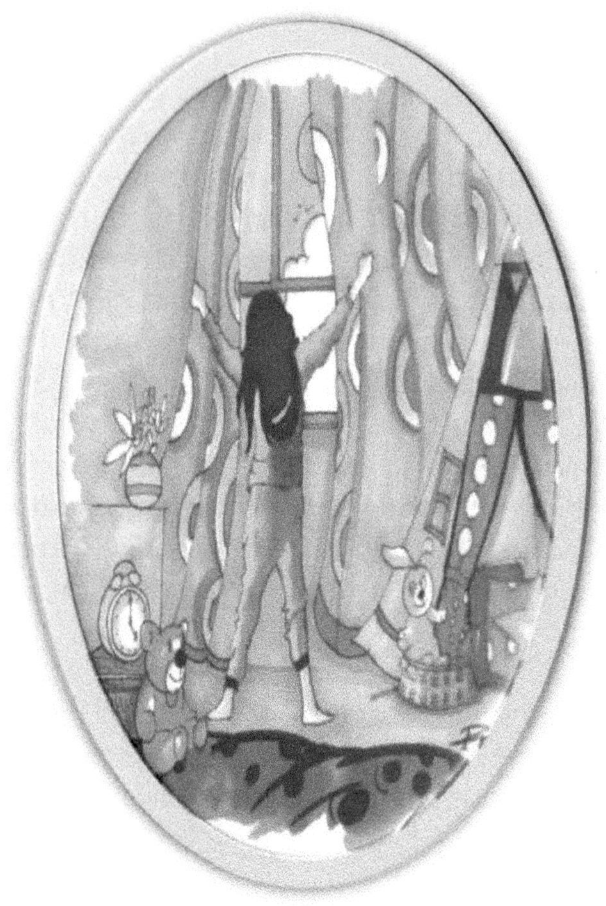

."Nothing is more beautiful than nature in the morning." (vincent van Gogh)

Waking up early is the greatest blessing one can give himself. Nature is at its best when it showers in the morning. It improves not only physical efficiency but also mental and emotional health.

According to research, early morning wake-up aids in better brain functioning, critical thinking, and problem-solving abilities. People who wake up early are filled with high energy and positive thinking. Early sleep and rising improve concentration and memory power. "The 5 AM Club" by Robin Sharma advocates greatly how waking up early using the 20/20/20 formula can change life from ordinary life to an exceptional life.

Jacqueline Lane, professor at Massachusetts General Hospital, published her findings in the *Nature Communications* journal, revealing *that early risers are happier and healthier and are at a lower risk of developing depression and chronic illnesses."* Individuals who tend to be happier tend to be morning-type individuals," Lane said.

Study published in the journal JAMA Psychiatry asserts that waking up early can reduce the risk of a person suffering from depression by 23 percent.

At my low points of life, when life seemed to slip off my hands, the first thing to turn around my life, to take control back, and drive it in my own way rather than being driven by it. I consciously work on my routine. The first thing is to wake up early. It has worked for me every time and my life has turned around from a curse to a blessing. Soon, everything starts to change drastically, and the life that had slipped from me comes back into my control. Once again, I become master of my destiny. It works in the first place with my thought process. I become calmer, at peace, and connected with myself. This peace empowers my mind, and my body feels energetic and fresh. Eventually, my efficiency improves, and my achievements increase. irrespective of the situation. My deadlines are met earlier than expected, and my goals are met as planned, as if body, mind, and soul are aligned and attuned with nature, moving in the best direction possible.

In my high school, I scored higher than my peers, despite their working longer hours. Some of them would ask me, "When do you study?" You are always playing around, chatting, never tense about studies or exams. The secret was an early morning wake-up. In the morning, the brain works at its best. I get more free hours during the day, more time for leisure.

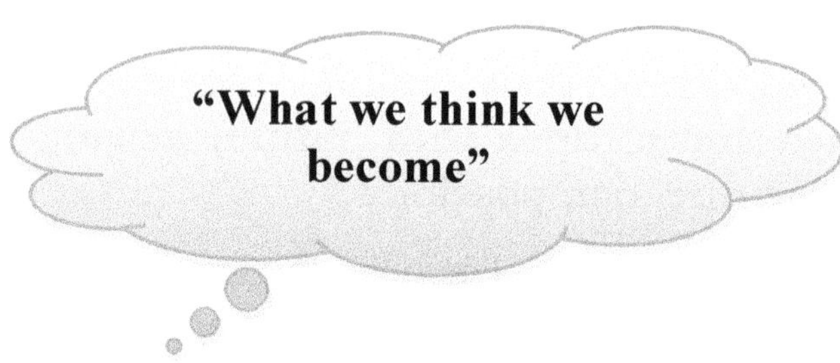

Thoughts are the basis or foundation of behavior; they are the seeds, and behavior is the fruit of the seeds (thoughts).We can fake our behavior, but not our thoughts. Thoughts are the first step that will be converted to action sooner or later, for long-term, effective results. Thoughts should be managed well. The behavior will be managed automatically.

Dr. Girish Patel, a psychiatrist from Mumbai, India, classifies thoughts into categories. Identify your thoughts and manage them well.

1. Toxic thoughts (like anger, anxiety, and the release of toxic chemicals)
2. Degrading—hurt, vengeance, jealousy—remains in the mind much

longer and is more harmful than toxic thoughts.

3. Automatic-could be positive or negative
4. Waste—unnecessary, insignificant
5. necessary, such as taking a bath or following a daily routine.
6. The 6 negative-negative thinker seeks out negativity in any situation or event.
7. Positive: the more favorable aspect of any situation
8. High-level Thoughts—Wisdom

Choose your thoughts wisely. Dr. Joseph Murphy, in his book "The Power of the Sub-Conscious Mind," asserts that "you are the sum total of your own thoughts; the way to overcome a negative thought is to substitute a good thought. Affirm the good, and the bad will vanish. "

We, society, education systems, and training, place a lot of emphasis on behaviors, and a lot of resources are invested in expected outcomes, but very little attention is paid to thought management because managing behavior without managing thoughts is just an outward manifestation of behavior.

A ritual, like wearing expensive clothes and jewelry without taking a bath, or ignoring inner cleanliness, may serve for a while, or maybe a very specific event when one is successful in fooling another, but results cannot be delivered in the long term. It is as good as acquiring training on sensitivity, but if you are not sensitive or compassionate, how long will that work?Knowing the formula of water does not quench the thirst. The approach has to be inward-outward rather than outward-in.

We have to choose either to "drive your life or life will drive you".

Osho, in his book called "Awareness", reveals the secret to becoming the master of his own life and destiny is by gaining consciousness, mastery of being alert and watchful to our thoughts. According to him, it is a step-by-step process where in the first step we become conscious of our body, like eating and walking. When we eat, enjoy every bite, and feel everything going on in the present. "Be in the present moment". As he continued with his sermon, he would do it and then stop when he realized he was being watched.

Finally, Buddha asked him why he did that. And he said he did it unconsciously; he was not even aware that he did it unconsciously. When he gained consciousness of his body, he was more aware of his body. The same applies to us. When we eat in front of the TV or while talking, we are not conscious of it. We are just putting something inside our bellies to stuff them. We are not taking care of the kind of energy we are using along with the food and water. We were walking on the road unaware, lost in the mobile, and an accident was just about to take place.

OSHO believes that to gain consciousness, the first step is body consciousness. Once body consciousness is achieved, the next step is thought consciousness. The third is consciousness towards feelings and emotions, where emotional intelligence arises.

Be in the Present Moment

UNDERSTAND ABOUT MULTIPLE INTELLIGENCES

https://youtu.be/lliU5KXBjBE

The American cognitive psychologist Howard Gardner presented "The Theory of Multiple Intelligences" (1983). His theory challenged the conventional belief that there is one single type of intelligence.

Gardner introduced eight different types of intelligence:

1. Linguistic terms
2. Logical /Mathematical
3. Spatial
4. Bodily-Kinaesthetic
5. Musical
6. Interpersonal
7. Intra-personal
8. Naturalist

Gardner introduced eight different types of intelligence:

1. Linguistic terms
2. Logical /Mathematical
3. Spatial
4. Bodily-Kinaesthetic
5. Musical
6. Interpersonal
7. Intra-personal
8. Naturalist

The linguistic and logical-mathematical types have been the most used in schools and society so far. The concept of emotional intelligence has been derived from Gardner's theory of multiple intelligences.

The concept of emotional intelligence has been derived from multiple intelligence.

A report card, which denotes only marks in certain subjects and linguistic and mathematical intelligence, is widely adopted by the education system. On the basis of limited abilities and intelligence, how can a report card conclude about a person's potential? Unfortunately, many students develop poor self-concepts because their report cards indicate poor grades, which affect the behaviours of the people around them.

People's attitudes tend to be negatively biased towards them in comparison to those who are doing better. Teachers tend to give more attention to those students in the class who are already doing well, and such students are neglected, which further empowers their poor self-concept. The attitude of their peers, and parents are not always supportive.

Their self-esteem suffers, Poor self-esteem can cause lifetime damage, not just sitting back in the class. It affects self-efficacy and, eventually, performance in academia, other activities in school, and later life. achieving goals and success in life. You must be aware and careful that the report card of the subject is not the report card of life. You are the architect of your life. Believe in yourself and trust yourself even when no one else does.

The Story of the Eagle and the Chickens

The story is about an eagle who thought she was a chicken. The farmer accidentally mixed up the eggs of the eagle and chicken. The eagle was raised with the rest of the chickens and believed himself to be a chicken and behaved like the chickens around him.

The eagle grew up doing what chickens do, living like a chicken, and believing he was a chicken. One day, the eagle and its chicks saw an eagle flying in the sky. They were mesmerized by the bird's flight, so high and wide that it seemed so powerful. The Eagle asked the other chicks, struck in awe, "Who is that in the sky? The chicks answered that an eagle is a kind of bird, very powerful. What a flight, the other chicks said. The other chick says, "that is an eagle." We are not even meant for such flights; we are meant for the earth. An eagle who mistook herself for a chick, strutting around the chicken coop, pecking at the ground, and acting like a chicken.

Though the villagers around her were surprised to see an eagle behaving like a chicken, they asked the farmer, who explained that now the eagle is no more an eagle but a chicken due to her training, and he also believes that. Eagle never actually tried or tapped her full potential. She believed her peers were chickens and never questioned that belief, and never dared to dream what was actually very natural to her. Her life could be much more. Many of us have similar stories to that of an eagle. We do not want to think beyond the box. We set our ambitions and choose careers based on the people around us without actually checking our potential. We don't respect our uniqueness. We tried very hard to fit it into the box. Maybe that box was not meant for you. Maybe you need a bigger box. Steve Jobs was often criticized for not fitting into the box because he needed a bigger box, so he created one for himself.

BALANCE YOUR VIRTUAL LIFE AND THE LIFE OF YOUR EXISTENCE

Social Media

Research proves that excessive social media usage is resulting in addiction and accounting for poor mental health; anxiety and depression have become the common outcomes. Spending long hours, ideally in a passive state, does not only make you lazy but is also not good for your health. Your creativity reduces, and less human interaction deprives one's social needs. A virtual platform creates an illusion of a world around you, but it is just superficial.

Escapism: Virtual platforms are great tools to escape. If you are not able to interact with people around you, it is very easy to interact virtually. Your problem did not go away; it was just a quick fix, a shortcut; you just did not face your problem and work on it.

People are trying to fill the void in their lives, which is again an illusion. If you feel lonely, how convenient it is to just start gazing at your cell phone, check FB, Instagram, or post a picture that attracts attention and you get so many likes, vows, and comments. It seems like a perfect solution. but it is no solution. You have to spend more time with yourself.

Create self-awareness, and find ways to have a fulfilling life. *No one will spend time with you if you don't do it yourself.*

If you don't like yourself, how in the world are others going to like you? Be your friend first; you will have the friends you need. If you are not your own friend, you are not ready to have the friends you need.

> *No One will spend time with you*
>
> *If you don't do it with your-self*

There are no shortcuts to a fulfilling life.

Engage yourself in creative activities that you like that transform your low energy into high energy, a state of positivity, constructiveness, and new learning.

My daughter was a very active, high-energy child, a cheerful child. Soon, TV became the most important member of the family, providing a distraction from the current issue, to which we had no clear solution or, indeed, much hope. Beginning with "Ramayana" on Netflix, it was for us adults. My daughter now watches not only an hour of cartoons but begins with movies like "Heidi, frozen, and YouTube." Of course, now the hours of watching have increased manifold. Her online school classes began, which came as a relief. At least she has a few hours.

When she could interact and have a proper routine Soon, I noticed her symptoms of anxiety and depression. I was on alert; she had switched to secretly watching meme videos, which were not good for her, and playing online games. She was an addict now. Being a sensitive child, I had to be even more careful. I began spending more time with her, persuading her to do a few activities with me.

I knew it would take time, and she needed more love, attention, and patience. I engaged her with her hobby classes, like music and dance, and motivated her to do what she really likes and be creative. After two weeks, I noticed a significant increase in positivity and energy.

- ❖ Allot time to daily activities in such a way that you find time for your hobbies, creativity, and physical fitness.
- ❖ Social media is a tool; don't become a slave to it.
- ❖ Don't use it for your boredom. Be creative. Be real. Find something interesting that gives you actual happiness, not an illusion of happiness.
- ❖ It cannot fill the void in your life. Don't even try it.
- ❖ Allot a fixed time for it and spend only that amount of time, not any time or every time.
- ❖ Never start your day with your mobile phone. That's the worst thing you can do to yourself.
- ❖ The morning is the most special part of the day that defines the quality of the rest of your day, and each day summed together defines your life and determines your destiny.
- ❖ Do not go to bed with your mobile phone. It not only radiates harmful vibrations. Before sleeping, whatever we do, our subconscious mind works

on that whole night. Trust me, it would exhaust you.

❖ Do not be automated or mechanical. Use social media as an instrument, don't be their instrument.

Masaru Emoto is a Japanese scientist and author of the book
"The Hidden Messages in Water," a New York Times bestseller. His experiments proved that human consciousness could affect the molecular structure of water. He describes in his book the relationship between water and human consciousness and thoughts.

> *Human beings are 99 percent water in foetuses, 90 percent when born, and around 70 percent in adulthood, and when dying in old age, it is around 50 percent water. He discovered a profound relationship between human vibrations, energy, sound, words, and existence with water.*

Human beings are 99 percent water in fetuses, 90 percent when born, around 70 percent in adulthood, and dying in old age is around 50 percent water. He discovered a profound relationship between human vibrations, energy, sound, words, and existence with water.The vibration of words has a surprisingly powerful influence on water. When positive words like "Thank you" and "Love" were written around a bottle of water, it resulted in the formation of beautiful clear crystals, while negative words like "you fool" and "you make me sick" ("You Fool") resulted in the formation of deformed, ugly crystal images. Similarly, water exposed to heavy metallic music and soothing music created very different crystals. The experiment proved a relationship between words and water. Because water makes up roughly 70% of our bodies, it is critical that we understand our relationship with it.

Impact of Love and Gratitude on Water

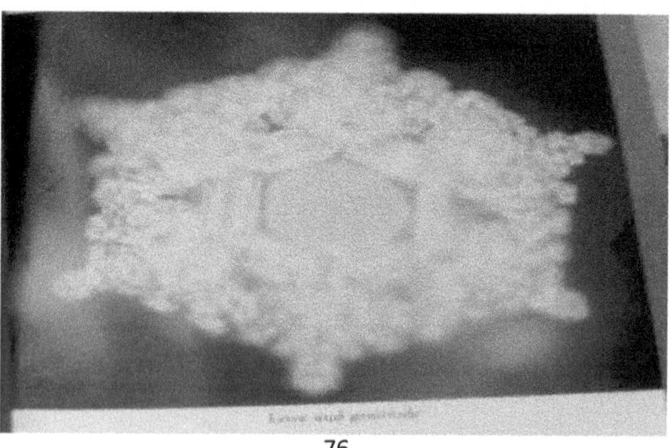

Masaru Emoto "The hidden messages of water" (2005) P5

It seemed as if the water was rejoicing and celebrating when it received positive words like love and gratitude. How much impact might it have on the human body, mind, and heart? Words have a powerful impact on the way we think and feel. By sending the right messages and saying positive words, our minds could be reconditioned to a higher state of mind, a higher consciousness.

Masaru Emoto "The hidden messages of water" (2005) P6

Water exposed to 'Thank You' resulted in the formation of beautiful crystals in hexagons.

These were distorted and ugly shapes of water crystals when water was exposed to negative words like "you fool." and "you make me feel sick. "negative words like "you fool.", "You make me feel sick"

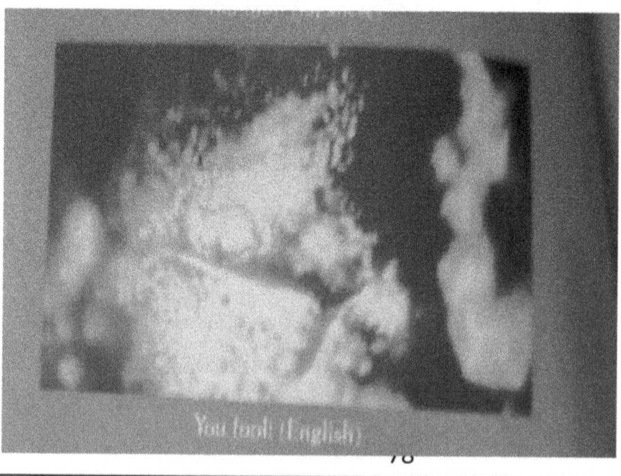

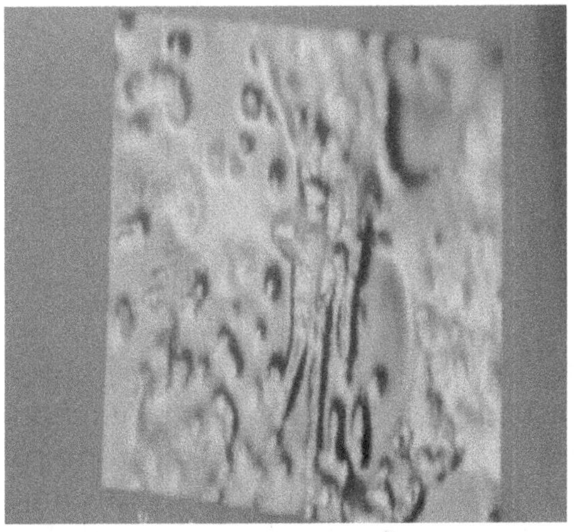

Masaru Emoto "The hidden messages of water" (2005) P 8

Similarly, pictures were shared by his study, which shows the varying impact of soothing and heavy metallic music on the water. When we say positive affirmations to ourselves like "I am worth it", "Let's do it", etc., it is well taken in the memory of water, so is the impact of negative thoughts and words.

Even though words are not spoken, they have vibrations that are taken by the water, and we humans, who are 70 percent water, can be impacted like the results of research by Masaru.

In Indian culture, a lot of emphasis is given to how and by whom food is cooked. It is believed that the state of mind of the person who is cooking is going to affect the energy and quality of the food. Emoto's research just validates the fact and offers a logic behind the belief. Many people may not be aware of the scientific research of Emoto, but in India, it is still followed and believed that when food is cooked, not only the physical hygiene of the surroundings is to be maintained but also the mental hygiene of the person cooking the food. It is further believed that when food is eaten, it should be noted not to be in the vicinity of noise, TV, or any discussion that contains low vibration. The Sanskrit phrase "YathaAahar-Tatha Vichaar," very much popular in Hindi, "jaisa Tan, waisa Man," is quite popular, which means food impacts the quality of thoughts.

SELF -LOVE

Have a long-life affair with your own self. Take charge of your best self on all levels: physical, mental, and emotional. Include exercise, yoga, dance, or anything that takes care of your physical being. Include a hobby. Surround yourself with positive people and people of high vibration. Stay away from toxic people and toxic relationships. Become more self-aware and conscious of yourself and your surroundings. Be assertive. Assertiveness, if served with diplomacy, can produce great results. Be grateful. Count your blessings before complaining. Love both yourself and others......What do we do when we love someone? We make an effort to make the individual happy. Shower him with valuable gifts. Make an effort to impress by being at your best. Accepting the person for who he is, with all his flaws, forgiving him over and over, we realize it's human. We enjoyed the company. We spent time with the person.

We respect him. Honesty is crucial. Support unconditionally.

What is our relationship with ourselves? Is it nourishing or poisonous? Whatever seed we water and plant will grow and produce the same results. It is a law of nature. Newton's Third Law states: "For every action, there is an equal and opposite reaction."What you sow, so you reap.

The Theory of "Karma" has been believed in by Indian Hindu families forever. It is part of our belief system. The same is true for you. Whatever we give ourselves, knowingly or unknowingly, has an effect on us. This is becoming our karma. The same outcome will be there. Take care of your physical being. Include a hobby.

PRINCIPLES OF SELF - RELATIONSHIP

Accept yourself first. Others will accept you

(even if they don't, it is not your responsibility to fix it).

Respect yourself.

Be your own priority.

Support yourself unconditionally.

Be honest with yourself.

Don't keep others' garbage (judgments, opinions).

Stop hurting yourself (with painful memories, guilt, etc.).

Surround yourself with positive people and people of high vibration. When we invest ourselves in relationships with our own selves with all our heart and soul and nurture them regularly, such a relationship grows with time and keeps getting stronger...

- Remember, you are a blessing. Your life is a blessing. Don't let anything take away your right to happiness. It is your responsibility to look after your best interests.

- You are the master of your destiny, the architect of your life.

- Be wise to choose well.

- Don't be afraid of making mistakes. It is a sign that you are learning and growing. One has to get in the pool to learn to swim. You will be safe outside, but no learning will take place. Don't ignore your instincts. You are you. Think like you. Never forget to trust yourself.

- Don't try to please everyone; you will lose yourself in the process. Once you lose yourself, that is exactly when the fall begins, which is further deeper. Don't complain if others are not giving you what you want. You are not giving it to yourself, be it love or respect. Whatever you do, do it with all your heart and soul. Let it be your best shot. Do it for yourself, not to impress anyone. Excellence will follow you and you will have greater respect for yourself.

- Don't be a dustbin to others; don't keep other people's garbage (comments, opinions, judgments).

- Concentrate on yourself; become so preoccupied with your own construction that you have no time to waste your valuable time, energy, and emotions on other people's flaws. Whatever you focus on is going to grow.

- Spend quality time with yourself by engaging daily in at least one of your hobbies.

- Count your blessings every day. Many people do not have these things: life, food, shelter, a job, a family, an education, and time.

- Enjoy the journey. Don't wait for the destination to arrive; not only should the destination be beautiful, but so should the journey.

"Stop trying to impress people

Impress yourself

Stretch yourself

Test yourself

Be the best version of you that you can be"

(vexking, Good vibes Good life)

Love yourself, spread love.

ACKNOWLEDGMENT

- I extend my gratitude to divine forces who continue to align with my purpose in life and let me experience immense peace, happiness, and love, making my path and destination beautiful.

- My spiritual gurus are Sant Uma Devi Kalyani and Shri Ram Nivas Yadav.

- My family—parents for trusting me and showering an abundance of love; the two most beautiful girls; my sister Diksha, my daughter Saanvi, and my husband Shobhit for unconditional love and support.

- My colleague, Dr. Prem Kumar, for his constant support and motivation.

- My mentors, Professor Leszek Cichoblazinski and Dr. Pradeep Biswas, for motivating me towards research and academics
- My boss, Dr. Inderjeet Dagar, was always encouraging and provided the required cooperation.

REFERENCES

- Baron & Misra.(2016).*Psychology. Pearson India Education Services Pt.Ltd, India, P 244-273.*
- *Blumenthal. Karen (2012). Steve Jobs. Bloomsbury Publishing, New Delhi, India. P191*
- *Goleman.Daniel.(2013)Emotional Intelligence. Bloomsbury Publishing, New Delhi, India, p19-20*
- *Murphy. Joseph (2012). The power of your Subconscious Mind. Embassy Book Distributor.*
- *Peck Scott .M ((2006).The Road Less Travelled. Penguin Random House, UK.*
- *Sharma. Robbins (2018).The 5 AM club. Jaico Publishing House, Mumbai, India,p219*
- *Osho.(2001) Awareness The key to living in balance. Osho International Foundation.*
- *Emoto. Masuru.(2004).The hidden messages in water. Atria Books, New York.*
- *Vex king.(2018).Good Vibes Good Life. Hay House Publishers, India*
- *Darrisaw.Michelle.*Morning People Really Are Happier, According to Science (yahoo.com)*2019*